ELMHURST PUBLIC LIBRARY

3 1135 01964 4308

Kankakee Public Library
304 S. Indiana Avenue
Kankakee, IL 60901-3844

J
590
Jac

SUPER Animal Powers
The Amazing Abilities of Animals

Written by Ryan Jacobson, Photographs by Stan Tekiela

Adventure Publications
Cambridge, Minnesota

ELMHURST PUBLIC LIBRARY
125 S. Prospect Avenue
Elmhurst, IL 60126-3298

Dedication

For Lora and Anna, my two favorite kindergarten teachers. —Ryan Jacobson

Acknowledgements

A very special thank you to Jonathan Norberg for a book design that truly lives up to the word "super." Thank you to Andrea Bong and her son Ethan for lending us your chameleon, Stuart, for a day. Thank you to Molly Merkle for letting me run with this idea and to Brett Ortler for your input. Thank you to Aaron Wells for your horned lizard expertise. Finally, thank you, Jonah and Lucas, for being my test readers. —RJ

Credits

Edited by Sandy Livoti

Illustrations by Phil Juliano

Cover and book design by Jonathan Norberg

All photos by Stan Tekiela except for the following: Tom Murray: 7 (all); Jonathan Norberg: backcover, 22–23 (main, upper left); Shutterstock: spine, 2–3 (all), 8–9 (lower left, upper right), 16–17 (upper left, lower right), 18–19 (upper left and right, lower left), 20–21 (upper left, lower right, main), 22–23 (upper left, lower left and right), 24–25 (main), 26–27 (main), 28–29 (upper left), 30–31 (all)

Copyright 2016 by Ryan Jacobson and Stan Tekiela
Published by Adventure Publications
820 Cleveland Street South
Cambridge, Minnesota 55008
(800) 678-7006
www.adventurepublications.net
All rights reserved
Printed in China
ISBN: 978-1-59193-648-0; eISBN: 978-1-59193-663-3

You can do amazing things—like see, hear, smell and move. But you can't do them as well as some animals. They have abilities that can only be described as super! Of course, your SUPER POWER IS YOUR BRAIN. You're smarter than all the wildlife in this book! Use your super power to learn what these incredible critters can do.

Up next...

WHICH ANIMAL HAS SUPER SPEED? ▶

The Peregrine Falcon

The fastest animal in the world doesn't run like a wolf. It soars through the sky! Peregrine Falcons can fly more than **200 MILES PER HOUR.** They use that speed to hunt. When a falcon sees a small bird, it zooms toward its prey. The falcon strikes with its feet. Then it loops around and grabs the bird as it falls toward the ground.

What if you had the Peregrine Falcon's super speed? You would be as fast as a race car!

Up next...

WHICH ANIMAL IS SUPER STRONG?

You might guess that the world's strongest animal is a bear. But bears are wimps compared to the mighty Dung Beetle! Now, this doesn't mean a Dung Beetle can lift more than a bear can. But a Dung Beetle is stronger for its size than a bear is for its size. Some Dung Beetles can pull the weight of 1,141 OTHER DUNG BEETLES. A bear can only lift about one other bear.

What if you had super strength like a Dung Beetle? You could carry a bus to school!

The Dung Beetle

Up next...

WHAT MAMMAL WEARS A SUIT OF ARMOR?

The Nine-Banded Armadillo

What if you had armor like an armadillo? It wouldn't hurt to fall off your bike!

Small critters need protection from animals that eat them, like foxes and coyotes. Lucky for the Nine-Banded Armadillo, it's covered with armor. **BONY PLATES** shield an armadillo's head, back, sides, legs and tail. This makes an armadillo very hard to bite. Those foxes and coyotes will have to find their dinner somewhere else!

Up next...

WHICH ANIMAL IS A SUPER THIEF? ▶

What if you took food like a Northern Raccoon does? You'd get into big trouble!

Northern Raccoons love to eat. Their favorite food is . . . just about anything. And they'll do just about anything to get it! Raccoons are SMART AND VERY SNEAKY. They can swim, climb, crawl and run. They have been known to take food from tents, garages, houses and even restaurants. These little critters look like they're wearing a mask!

The Northern Raccoon

Up next...

WHICH ANIMAL HAS SUPER VISION? ▶

What if you had a Golden Eagle's super vision? You could spot a bread crumb from across the gym!

The Golden Eagle

Has anyone ever said you have "eagle eyes"? It means you can see really well. This saying comes straight from the animal kingdom. Eagles have super vision! When an eagle hunts, it flies high in the sky, and it still sees its prey. An eagle can spot small animals, like rabbits, on the ground from **THREE MILES AWAY.**

Up next...

WHAT MAMMAL CAN SUPER SMELL?

What if you super-smelled like a Black Bear? You could tell what a person was cooking for dinner—in a different town!

Super smell may sound like a boring power. But it comes in handy for Black Bears. These giant critters love to eat. Too bad for them, they aren't great hunters. They fill their bellies by finding food. Black Bears can smell their favorite treats—like berries, fish and meat—across a whole forest. Some people think their noses work from AS FAR AWAY AS 20 MILES.

The Black Bear

Up next...

WHAT REPTILE HAS A SUPER SIXTH SENSE? ▶

The **Pit Viper**

What if you sensed heat like a Pit Viper? You could play tag in the dark!

Most animals have five senses: hearing, sight, smell, taste and touch. But some snakes use a unique sixth sense: the ABILITY TO DETECT HEAT. Warm-blooded creatures—such as mice, rabbits and even you—always give off heat. Pit Vipers' heat-sensing powers help them to find small critters to eat, even if those critters are hiding.

Up next...

WHICH BIRD IS SUPER TRICKY? ▶

The Northern Mockingbird

What if you could sing like a mockingbird? You'd sound like all of your favorite music stars!

What do you hear? The sounds of many different birds? You might not be hearing other birds at all. A Northern Mockingbird could be tricking you! These birds "mock" or mimic other songs. In fact, they can learn UP TO 200 DIFFERENT SONGS. They sing to show off for other mockingbirds and to find themselves a mate.

Up next...

WHICH ANIMAL FLINGS DARTS AT ITS ENEMIES?

What if you had barbed hair like a Tarantula? Even bullies would be afraid of you!

Some famous heroes fight crime with bows and arrows. Tarantulas have weapons, too: barbed hairs. These hairs cover the back of a Tarantula. When the spider senses danger, it **RUBS HAIRS OFF ITS BACK.** The hairs float into the air and get into the other animal's skin or eyes. Usually, the pain scares the animal away.

The Tarantula

Up next...

WHICH ANIMAL CAN TURN INVISIBLE? ▶

The Chameleon

Chameleons are small lizards. Larger animals, like birds and snakes, eat them. Chameleons aren't super strong, and they aren't super fast. How do they survive? By hiding! Chameleons can't really turn invisible, but they come close. Many types of chameleons **CHANGE THEIR SKIN COLOR** to match their surroundings.

What if you could disappear like a chameleon? You could hide when you get in trouble!

Up next...

WHAT MAMMAL HAS SUPER HEARING? ▶

The Bat

What if you had a bat's super hearing? You could catch a ball with your eyes closed!

Bats hunt for insects at night. Of course, hunting in the dark is hard, so it's a good thing bats' ears are super. They have a **POWER CALLED ECHOLOCATION** (eck-oh-low-kay-shun). The bats make a whole bunch of squeaking noises that we can't hear. The squeaks hit objects and bounce back, or echo. When bats hear the echoes, they can tell where things are, even if it's too dark to see.

Up next...

WHICH BIRD IS STEALTHY LIKE A NINJA? ▶

Ninjas are quiet, crafty and great at hiding. Owls are the ninjas of the animal kingdom. Many owls do their best hunting at night, thanks to their super hearing and their ability to **FLY WITHOUT MAKING A SOUND.** Owls hide in places like trees or barns. They have been known to puff up or slim down their bodies in order to blend with their surroundings.

What if you were stealthy like an owl? You would be a hide-and-seek champion!

The Owl

Up next...

WHAT MOUNTAIN MAMMAL IS A SUPER CLIMBER?

The Mountain Goat

Mountain Goats live in the mountains. There, they keep away from animals that would eat them, like bears and cougars. Mountain Goats use their super climbing skills to move around on rocky cliffs and ledges. They have STRONG LEGS AND GREAT BALANCE. Plus, their special hooves help them cling to rocks and boulders.

What if you could climb like a Mountain Goat? You could go upstairs—without using the stairs!

Up next...

WHICH ANIMAL HAS LASER EYES? ▶

Horned Lizards don't really shoot lasers from their eyes. They do something even cooler! They are as small as toads, which makes them look tasty to other animals. If a lizard is about to be eaten, it squirts blood from its eyes! The blood shoots **AS FAR AS THREE FEET,** and that confuses other animals. Plus, the blood tastes awful, which might help the lizard to get away.

What if you had eyes like a Horned Lizard? At your size, the blood would squirt all the way across a classroom!

The Horned Lizard

Up next...

WHAT ANIMALS CAN MAKE BOOKS? ▶

ABOUT THE AUTHOR

Ryan Jacobson is an author and presenter. He has written more than 40 books, priding himself on telling high-interest stories for each age level. He can talk picture books in kindergarten, ghost stories in eighth grade and other fun stuff in between. Ryan has performed at countless schools and special events. For more about the author, visit AuthorRyanJacobson.com.

ABOUT THE PHOTOGRAPHER

Stan Tekiela is an award-winning naturalist, wildlife photographer and writer. He has authored more than 140 field guides, nature books, children's books and wildlife audio CDs, presenting many species of birds, mammals, reptiles, amphibians, trees, wildflowers and cacti. In addition, he writes a syndicated column about nature, which appears in over 25 cities across eight states.